She Persisted

ELLA FITZGERALD

—INSPIRED BY—

She Persisted

by Chelsea Clinton & Alexandra Boiger

· ·

ELLA FITZGERALD

· ·

Written by
Andrea Davis Pinkney

Interior illustrations by
Gillian Flint

PHILOMEL

PHILOMEL BOOKS
An imprint of Penguin Random House LLC, New York

First published in the United States of America by Philomel Books,
an imprint of Penguin Random House LLC, 2023

Text copyright © 2023 by Chelsea Clinton.
Illustrations copyright © 2023 by Alexandra Boiger.

Philomel Books is a registered trademark of Penguin Random House LLC.

Visit us online at penguinrandomhouse.com.

Library of Congress Cataloging-in-Publication Data is available.

Printed in the United States of America

HC ISBN 9780593620878
10 9 8 7 6 5 4 3 2 1

PB ISBN 9780593620885
10 9 8 7 6 5 4 3 2 1

WOR

Edited by Talia Benamy and Jill Santopolo.
Design by Ellice M. Lee.
Text set in LTC Kennerley Pro.

∾ To ∽
Gwennie and Gloria,
who make so many hearts sing!

She
Persisted

....

She Persisted: MARIAN ANDERSON

She Persisted: VIRGINIA APGAR

She Persisted: PURA BELPRÉ

She Persisted: SIMONE BILES

She Persisted: NELLIE BLY

She Persisted: RUBY BRIDGES

She Persisted: KALPANA CHAWLA

She Persisted: CLAUDETTE COLVIN

She Persisted: ELLA FITZGERALD

She Persisted: ROSALIND FRANKLIN

She Persisted: TEMPLE GRANDIN

She Persisted: DEB HAALAND

She Persisted: BETHANY HAMILTON

She Persisted: DOROTHY HEIGHT

She Persisted: FLORENCE GRIFFITH JOYNER

She Persisted: HELEN KELLER

She Persisted: CORETTA SCOTT KING

She Persisted: CLARA LEMLICH

She Persisted: RACHEL LEVINE

She Persisted: MAYA LIN

She Persisted: WANGARI MAATHAI

She Persisted: WILMA MANKILLER

She Persisted: PATSY MINK

She Persisted: FLORENCE NIGHTINGALE

She Persisted: SALLY RIDE

She Persisted: MARGARET CHASE SMITH

She Persisted: SONIA SOTOMAYOR

She Persisted: MARIA TALLCHIEF

She Persisted: DIANA TAURASI

She Persisted: HARRIET TUBMAN

She Persisted: OPRAH WINFREY

She Persisted: MALALA YOUSAFZAI

Dear Reader,

As Sally Ride and Marian Wright Edelman both powerfully said, "You can't be what you can't see." When Sally said that, she meant that it was hard to dream of being an astronaut, like she was, or a doctor or an athlete or anything at all if you didn't see someone like you who already had lived that dream. She especially was talking about seeing women in jobs that historically were held by men.

I wrote the first *She Persisted* and the books that came after it because I wanted young girls—and children of all genders—to see women who worked hard to live their dreams. And I wanted all of us to see examples of persistence in the face of different challenges to help inspire us in our own lives.

I'm so thrilled now to partner with a sisterhood of writers to bring longer, more in-depth versions of these stories of women's persistence and achievement to readers. I hope you enjoy these chapter books as much as I do and find them inspiring and empowering.

And remember: If anyone ever tells you no, if anyone ever says your voice isn't important or your dreams are too big, remember these women. They persisted and so should you.

Warmly,
Chelsea Clinton

ELLA FITZGERALD

TABLE OF CONTENTS

....

·····························

CHAPTER 1

Twinkle Child

Ella Jane Fitzgerald was born with her own special rhythm. Like every new baby, she let out a cry to show the world she'd arrived. It was April 25, 1917, when this beautiful child blinked hello. Newport News, Virginia, the town where Ella was born, rested between the James River and Chesapeake Bay. Ella's mother, Tempie, and her father, William, must have seen the wide-open hope of possibility when they looked into their new baby's eyes.

Even as an infant, Ella was feisty. That little girl wriggled, kicked, and gurgled with a sure might. And like the river and bay that glistened along the banks of her hometown, Ella had a twinkle, too.

Not long after Ella was born, her parents parted ways. Ella and Tempie packed up, waved goodbye to Virginia, and moved to Yonkers, New York, where a new life waited for them. As she grew up, Ella made friends quickly. She was strong and quick. When the neighborhood kids gathered to play baseball, Ella was there, ready to swing a bat, pitch, and race around the bases.

Tempie worked as a laundress. When Ella's mother was busy folding clothes and hanging sheets to dry, Ella hung out with her friends. Ella

and the other girls in her neighborhood taught
themselves to pretty-step. To move their feet
on the sidewalks and streets. To dance for the
Yonkers city folk who passed by. Ella had her
own one-of-a-kind way of moving. Her dancing

was filled with lots of determination. The concrete slabs were Ella's stage. Imagination was her spotlight.

When Ella was a teenager, her mother passed away after being in car accident. This was very hard for Ella. She struggled in school, and sometimes misbehaved in her classes. Ella's father couldn't be found, so she was sent by the state to live in a place called a reform school, where, back in the 1930s, children with troubles and no family were made to stay.

The one bright spot in Ella's life at that time was her passion for dancing. Ella's neighbors suggested that she and her friends get on the local train and take her hoofin' to Harlem, the New York City hotspot, where Black talent glistened on every corner. Harlem was home to poets, performers, speakers, preachers, and anybody who had the grit and will to show off their creative skills. In Harlem, if you had an artistic gift to share, folks were eager to rise up and meet it.

After school, Ella was often on that sixty-minute train ride to the big city. The place where her dance dreams could come true.

In time, Harlem became Ella's stomping ground. On November 21, 1934, Ella entered a talent contest at the Apollo Theater, a famous theater where many performers got their start. She was ready to dance her way to fame. But as soon as the stage announcer called Ella's name, and she looked out at the audience, whose faces were lit by a bunch of flickering floodlights, Ella froze. Her knees locked. Her neck started to sweat. It didn't help that her work boots and

hand-me-down clothes were nothing like the fancy dresses and bows worn by the other hopeful performers. Like Ella, they were there to impress.

Before Ella could even try a simple shuffle-step, the audience started to boo loudly. This was a tradition at the Apollo. If an act couldn't cut it, the performer could expect loud hisses and lots of heckling. But Ella had not come all this way to go home without a prize. That's when Ella quietly willed her rattling knees to knock it off. When she recalled that night years later, Ella said, "I looked and I saw all those people, and I said, 'Oh my gosh, what am I going to do . . . ? Everybody started laughing and said, 'What is she gonna do?' And I couldn't think of nothing else, so I tried to sing 'The Object of My Affection.'"

And, oh, did Ella belt! From somewhere deep

inside, that tune rose up and out and over all those boos and hisses. The audience got to their feet and brought on the applause.

Ella won the talent contest. That night, she came to an understanding that changed her life forever. Dancing had encouraged her to try. But singing would let her fly!

....

Shy Girl Standing Tall

S axophonist Benny Carter was in the band during Ella's performance at the Apollo Theater. Benny was impressed with Ella's natural singing abilities. After the show, he began introducing Ella to people in the entertainment business who could help her get more chances to sing. Ella entered other talent contests, and she kept winning!

Even though Ella was getting noticed by band leaders, she remained very shy. Offstage and with people she didn't know, Ella didn't talk much. When she wasn't performing, Ella sometimes compared herself to well-known singers and wondered if she had enough skill to make it as a performer. One elegantly dressed singer named Billie Holiday was beginning to come onto the scene and was getting noticed by audiences and record companies.

Ella secretly worried about her own singing talent and the way she looked. She still didn't have sparkly costumes and a styled hairdo like the other ladies she saw performing. This made her doubt her abilities before walking onto the stage.

But every time Ella got in front of an audience, her doubts disappeared.

The spotlight seemed to melt her worries. She lifted her head, pulled back her shoulders, stood tall, and *sang.* "Once up there, I felt the acceptance and love from my audience," Ella said. "I knew I wanted to sing before people the rest of my life." With self-confidence guiding the way, Ella won the chance to sing at the Harlem Opera House as a featured vocalist. She performed with the Tiny Bradshaw Band, a well-known jazz orchestra. It was

January 1935. On that night, Bardu Ali, the master of ceremonies, knew Ella was a gifted singer. He was eager to introduce Ella to jazz drummer Chick Webb, the head of the Chick Webb Orchestra.

Bardu Ali also knew that Chick could be finicky. Chick was a hard-to-please dude. He liked his jazz music hotter than Tabasco sauce. Chick believed that when folks came to nightclubs, they were mostly there to hear the trombones, saxophones, and backbeat from the drums. Chick was known to have an attitude about vocalists. To his way of thinking, singers were far from the main attraction at a nightclub. Chick's view was, *Why pay a ticket to hear some singer, when it was instruments that brought the pulse to a party?* Besides, Chick had already hired a singer named Charlie Linton.

Well, Chick's stubborn ideas didn't worry Bardu Ali much. And they sure didn't stop Ella. She was ready to sing past any bad attitude Chick threw in her direction.

By this time, Ella was eighteen years old, and her confidence had grown. When Chick told her he'd test her grit by letting her sing at a Yale University dance, Ella was excited. Chick gave Ella a challenge. If her singing could get the folks at Yale onto the dance floor, Chick would hire Ella as his band's lead singer. He said, "If the kids like her, she stays."

While most college students love to party, the crowd at Yale was known to be stiff. Hoity-toity. Too cool to cut loose. *Shakin'* it wasn't how they rolled at Yale. Ella had her work set out for her. Speaking of cutting, she now had to show

Chick what she could do by singing so well that she could make those Yalies "cut a rug," which, back then, was what folks called fast dancing.

Ella arrived at Yale determined to prove herself. At first, those Yale students were shier than shy. Even with Chick's drumming, the room was filled with dance duds! Ella started to sing. And sing. *And sing.* Her voice and its rhythms put wings on Chick's beats. Ella rolled out a tune that had more jam than a jelly doughnut. Soon, the Yale kids went from dance scaredy-cats to hip kitties. Their dance feet put more heat on that floor than a bucketful of scotch-bonnet pepper stew. Ella's voice had the whole place hoppin'! Jammin'! Slammin'!

And *bam*—Chick was convinced that Ella meant business. Before the night was even halfway through, Chick switched up his attitude. He welcomed Ella to his traveling band. She would earn $12.50 per week, which would be about $250 per week today. Their next stop would be the Savoy Ballroom, Harlem's high-class dance spot.

. . . .

CHAPTER 3

Savoy Superstar

The Savoy was known as "the world's most famous ballroom." That swanky nightclub hosted only the best singers. Honey, if you wanted to stomp at the Savoy, you'd better be prepared to bring some swing. That's just what Ella did.

One way folks knew a singer had skills was by how many people came onto the dance floor when the singer let loose on her vocals. It was one thing to sing good enough to get people out there high-tailing it. It was a whole 'nother thing to spread rhythms that were powerful enough to *keep* lots of feet moving all night long. At the Savoy, Ella's turned-up tune talent encouraged people to dance the Kangaroo Hop, the Suzy Q., and the Lindy Hop, some of the most popular dances at that time. Even shy cats came out to play whenever Ella sang.

Most Savoy singers stayed on the bandstand while performing. Not Ella. Once the crowd got to stompin', she came down from the stage and danced with the customers who'd paid a pretty penny to see her perform. Ella was humble. She remembered dancing on street corners. Being one among many was now her way of showing how much she cared about the paying customers who respected her talent.

During this time, around 1936, Chick Webb took Ella under his wing. Chick taught Ella how to bring out the best tones using the special voice she'd been born to share.

Each night's Savoy performance was broadcast live on the radio. This meant Ella's colorful voice was rising and spreading like a rainbow of sound. Ella could be heard from Brooklyn to Berkeley to Biloxi and back. Soon nightclub owners were waiting in line to invite Ella Fitzgerald to headline on their stages. Ella's singing took her listeners to Cloud Nine, and her velvety voice lifted Chick Webb's orchestra to new heights.

Producers were eager to record Ella's music. This would allow her fans to listen whenever they wanted and to enjoy Ella's singular sound from their living rooms. In 1938, Ella and Al Feldman, a member of Chick's orchestra, wrote and recorded a song called "A-Tisket, A-Tasket." That pretty-ditty nursery rhyme became an instant hit! Ella and Al's song tells the story of a child who drops a letter she'd written to her mommy. When the letter is scooped up by a little girlie who puts it in her pocket, then takes Ella's yellow basket, Ella tells it like it is—that itty-bitty basket was the joy of her life. And the song that made that basket come alive also brought happy finger snapping to everybody who listened to its melody and words. Fans called "A-Tisket, A-Tasket" a jitterbug spiritual. That's because the song lifted the spirits of anyone who listened to its snappy tune and words, delivered as only Ella could. "A-Tisket, A-Tasket" made Ella famous. She was now a star.

....

CHAPTER 4

Stepping Up to Scat's Challenge

Ella left Chick's band to start her own career as a singer. She wanted to expand her singing talents to reach even more people. Also, Ella wanted to learn about ways she could make her voice shine brighter. She met a jazz trumpeter named Dizzy Gillespie who showed Ella that her voice had a powerful instrument within it, just like his trumpet.

He encouraged Ella to try something new.

He took out his brass horn and *blew*. The sounds coming from that trumpet were fast and loud. Their rhythms were rich with backflips and flatted fifths. Dizzy told Ella her singing could be like his horn playing. They could make it up as they went along. Ella didn't need to stick to any sheet music or written words for a song. This was called scat singing—having fun with notes, just like a bird's wings play with the wind when it flits and flutters.

Even though scat was musical freedom, it wasn't easy. It took nerve and confidence to throw away your sheet music and go with the flow. Like a brave bird, scat was all about winging it. Scat required Ella to stand proudly, open up, and trust that whatever sounds come through her would be the music meant to rise up and out in

that moment. This excited Ella. Not many singers were fearless enough to step into a spotlight
without knowing what would happen when the
band started playing. But Ella had the courage to
leap into scat singing's challenge. And, goodness,
could Ella scat!

There were very few singers who could
scat-sing back then. Ella had a unique talent for

expressing jazz through her special voice. In 1946, Ella started touring with Dizzy Gillespie's band. At concerts, when Ella got to the mic, she often started by singing the smooth back-and-forth tones of straight-ahead music. This warmed up her audience. Once folks were feeling good and swaying to her swing, Ella quickly went into scat's syncopated locomotion.

When Ella's scat broke free, it unleashed flutter-beats that brought jazz music's fever to the room. If you liked snapping your fingers and shaking loose your toe jam, Ella's sound could introduce beats you didn't know were in your own two feet. *That* was *scat*. Delivered as only bold Ella Fitzgerald could.

While on tour with Dizzy's band, Ella traveled to cities and towns in many states. It was now the 1950s, a time when most public places, including theaters, kept Black people and white people separate. This was especially true in the Southern United States, where laws supported segregation that didn't allow Black people to go to the same restaurants, movie theaters, and nightclubs as white people. Segregation was cruel and unfair.

This was also a time when Black people were often ridiculed, spat on, and beaten—just because their skin was brown. The opposite of segregation was *integration*, which meant people of all races and skin colors could be together. But integration wasn't common in the South when Ella's fame was growing. Even to some of her most devoted white fans, listening to Ella sing on the radio and on recorded albums wasn't the same as allowing a Black singer to be in a room with white people.

Ella was beautiful and proud, but this didn't matter to people who believed in segregation.

One night in 1955, Ella and Dizzy were scheduled to perform at a club in Houston, Texas. Back then, Houston was a city that was segregated. Before Ella and Dizzy arrived, Ella's manager, Norman Granz, spoke to the club owners. It was Norman's job to schedule Ella's appearances and to make sure the club was prepared with all the right lights and sound equipment for Ella's show. He insisted Ella and Dizzy's show must include Black customers alongside white audience members. To drive home his point, Norman took down the signs on the bathroom doors that labeled the restrooms "Negro" for Black people and "White" for everyone else.

When Ella and Dizzy performed on the

first night, the audience applauded so loudly, you could hear the clapping all over town. But as soon as the show ended, the police stormed into Ella's and Dizzy's dressing rooms and arrested them. Because of the segregation laws, the police treated them like criminals—even though it was the club manager who had allowed Black and white people in the audience! They took Ella and Dizzy to the police station. Thankfully, Ella and Dizzy weren't harmed. Instead, the police officer asked for Ella's autograph!

She proudly wrote her name on his wrinkled piece of paper. Through her strength and bravery, Ella had opened the door for the next Black singer who would perform at that club.

CHAPTER 5
·····························

Ella and Marilyn Persist

By that night in 1955, Ella was a national star. Her records had sold thousands of copies. She had won awards. She had paved the way for others.

But Ella still had to fight against racism and prejudice. The white owners of the theaters and nightclubs where Ella wanted to perform didn't want to allow a Black performer onstage, and they didn't want Black and white people to mix in their audiences. But they were forced to think carefully about their backward beliefs. Wherever Ella sang, she brought in huge crowds who spent money to buy the tickets to see her. These fans also purchased food and drinks at the nightclubs and restaurants. This meant the owners of these places had lots of dollars coming into their cash-boxes, thanks to Ella's performances.

By preventing Ella from appearing because of her skin color, the club owners were also stopping the flow of money their businesses earned. It was hard to turn Ella away when they saw how much she helped raise their profits.

But some club owners were still stubborn bigots who held tight to their hateful ideas. The Mocambo nightclub in Los Angeles, California, was one of those segregated places. Even though

they had allowed a very few Black performers onto their stage in the past, they still mostly stuck to not allowing Black talent to perform. The Mocambo was located in heart of the city. Lots of big-name Hollywood people hung out there, night after night. Marilyn Monroe, a very famous actress and singer, was a frequent guest at the Mocambo. Whenever Marilyn showed up, so did photographers, fans, movie studio heads, and record company big shots.

Marilyn hated the racist ways of the club owners who wouldn't let Ella sing on their bandstands. She also wanted as many people as possible to experience Ella's remarkable talent and grace. Like Ella, Marilyn was determined to stand up against unfair treatment. One night in 1957, Marilyn called the Mocambo. She told the owners that if they let Ella Fitzgerald perform, she'd show up every night and sit in the front. The Mocambo owners were reluctant at first. But Marilyn's proposal was hard to turn down.

Marilyn pointed out a simple fact that the Mocambo managers couldn't deny. She told them what they already knew was true—that her presence at the Mocambo would bring big publicity attention. It would increase the club's popularity. Newspapers and magazines from all over world would show pictures of Marilyn at the Mocambo. As a result, the club owners would make more money from the increase in people coming to their clubs to get a look at Marilyn and laying out some cash for food and drinks while they enjoyed being in the same place as such a big movie star.

Marilyn was persuasive. She meant business.

The guys who ran the Mocambo were forced to listen. When they thought carefully about what Marilyn's idea could do for their wallets and pockets, they went from shaking their heads *no* to nodding *yes*. Marilyn, the Mocambo, and Ella struck a deal.

When Marilyn showed up on the first night, she was confident the reporters would ask her which singer she was there to see. She also knew that her presence would help bring a bright spotlight to Ella.

Marilyn's plan worked. Ella performed at the Mocambo. Photographers and reporters went wild when they saw Marilyn Monroe, but their attention quickly turned to Ella, who got standing ovations, cheers, and requests for *just one more song* as the show was ending each night.

Ella and Marilyn became friends. They proved that when women stick together, important changes can happen through their persistence. Years later, when remembering Marilyn Monroe, Ella said, "She was an unusual woman—a little ahead of her time."

During her performances at the Mocambo, Ella commanded respect. She showed the world that true stars twinkle in every sky!

· ·

CHAPTER 6

The First Lady of Song

Ella was unstoppable. After the Mocambo, she toured many cities in the United States and around the world. She dazzled audiences in nations all over the globe—singing, scatting, and speaking up about music's power to make the world a better place. During this time, America continued to face racial disharmony.

Ella had proven that music brought people together. She let concert organizers know she would only perform in front of integrated audiences. Concert halls were transformed by Ella's presence.

At the same time, Ella recorded the music of the most popular American composers. From the late 1950s through 1964, she created the Complete Ella Fitzgerald Song Books, a series of albums that celebrated the works of Irving Berlin, George and Ira Gershwin, Cole Porter, and others. Through these recordings, Ella showed that a Black singer could bring class, beauty, and widespread attention to the works of notable white composers. Ira Gershwin said, "I never knew how good our songs were until I heard Ella Fitzgerald sing them."

As Ella's career progressed, she worked hard to break down racial barriers and to end the

mistreatment of women and children. Ella sometimes made public appearances for young people,
reminding them of the importance of education
and fairness. She also let children know that they

could rejoice in their talents and feel confident in their abilities.

In addition to many honors and lifetime achievement awards that noted her talents and accomplishments as a singer, Ella received recognition for her work in speaking up about equal rights for Black people. She was awarded the National Association for the Advancement of Colored People (NAACP) Equal Justice Award and the American Black Achievement Award.

Ella's success kept growing. She donated some of the money she'd earned from her recordings to create the Ella Fitzgerald Charitable Foundation to help children of all races, cultures, and beliefs get proper medical care, housing, and education. Ella was especially focused on the importance of teaching kids to read, to enjoy music, and to reach for their dreams. She once said, "Just don't give up trying to do what you really want to do. Where there is love and inspiration, I don't think you can go wrong."

In 1979, Ella was honored at Washington, DC's Kennedy Center by President Jimmy Carter and First Lady Rosalynn Carter. As the host that night, Rosalynn named Ella one of the most

important American performers in history. President Ronald Reagan presented Ella with the 1987 National Medal of Arts. By this time, Ella had come to be known as "the First Lady of Song."

Ella Fitzgerald was a first in many ways. She performed in white-owned nightclubs at a time when Black singers were turned away. Ella was also among the first female performers to make scat singing a popular art form. And Ella was the first Black woman in history to win a Grammy Award, the highest honor given to people in the music industry.

Ella Fitzgerald died on June 15, 1996. But her brilliance has kept on shining. In 2007, the United States Postal Service honored Ella's memory with a postage stamp that showed her portrait. The stamp was part of the Postal Service's Black

Heritage series. Today there's even an Ella Fitzgerald Barbie Doll, which is part of the Barbie Inspiring Women Series that celebrates courageous women who took risks, changed rules, and paved the way. The one and only Ella Fitzgerald did all that and more!

HOW YOU CAN PERSIST

by Andrea Davis Pinkney

To celebrate Ella Fitzgerald's accomplishments, here are some activities to enjoy with friends and family:

1. Create an "A-Tisket, A-Tasket" basket. In keeping with the words of Ella's song, make sure the basket is yellow. On slips of paper, write down things that make

you happy, proud, and grateful. Fold the papers, and put them in the basket. Each week, reach into the basket, unfold one of the sheets, and share your "A-Tisket, A-Tasket" with a friend.

2. Host an Ella Fitzgerald birthday party on April 25 to celebrate the day Ella was born. Listen to her music, and enjoy a sing-along with your family or classmates.

3. Write about challenging situations you've gone through that were made better through your own creativity. Make a list of what you did to succeed. Share this list with a friend in need, and invite your friend to make a list of their own.

4. Ask a grandparent or elder to tell you about their favorite memories of hearing Ella's music when they were young. Draw pictures of the scenes that make up those remembrances. With your artwork, make an Ella memory book as a gift to these grown-ups.

5. Create your own Ella Fitzgerald postage stamp as inspiration for writing a letter to a friend, telling them why you love Ella Fitzgerald. Even though the stamp wouldn't be "official" postage for mailing the letter, you can hand-deliver the letter to your friend, singing the praises of your own postage stamp creation.

6. To express the importance of Ella being called "the First Lady of Song," and to rejoice in your own accomplishments, keep a journal of your hopes for becoming "the First Kid of _____."

Acknowledgments

It is with gratitude that I wish to thank the following people and institutions. To the Ella Fitzgerald Charitable Foundation, thank you for your tireless work on behalf of youth and women. Gratitude and admiration to Chelsea Clinton for showing the thought leaders of tomorrow that persisting brings change. Deep thanks to editors Jill Santopolo and Talia Benamy for your keen editorial brilliance and vision and for bringing heart and harmony to all that you do. To artists Alexandra Boiger and Gillian Flint, thank you for bringing Ella's life and times to young minds and eyes through your cover art and interior illustrations. To my agent, Rebecca Sherman, I extend ongoing thanks for always hitting the right notes. To my husband, Brian Pinkney, and children, Chloe and Dobbin, thank you for filling my heart with music.

∽ References ∾

BOOKS:

Gillespie, Dizzy, with Al Fraser. *To Be or Not to . . . Bop: Memoirs.* New York: Da Capo Press, 1979.

Hitchhock, Wiley H., and Stanley Sadie, eds. *The New Grove Dictionary of American Music.* New York: Grove Dictionaries of Music, 1986.

Kliment, Bud. *Ella Fitzgerald: First Lady of American Song.* New York: Chelsea House Publishers, 1988.

Nicholson, Stuart. *Ella Fitzgerald: A Biography of the First Lady of Jazz.* New York: Charles Scribner's Sons, 1994.

Pinkney, Andrea Davis. *Ella Fitzgerald: The Tale of a Vocal Virtuosa.* New York: Hyperion Books for Children, Inc., 2002

Wyman, Carolyn. *Ella Fitzgerald: Jazz Singer Supreme.* New York: Franklin Watts, 1993.

FILMS:

Ella Fitzgerald: Something to Live For. American Masters Series. Public Broadcasting Service, 1999.

Forever Ella. A&E Television Networks, 1999.

Jazz Classics—Harlem Harmonies, vol I. 1940–1945. Rahway, N.J.: Videofidelity, 1986.

Jazz Classics—Harlem Harmonies, vol. II. 1941–1946. Rahway, N.J.: Amvest Video, 1987.

SELECTED DISCOGRAPHY

Ella and Louis (Verve Records)

Ella Fitzgerald Sings the Cole Porter Songbook (Verve Records)

Ella Fitzgerald Sings the George and Ira Gershwin Songbook (Verve Records)

Ella in Berlin (Verve Records)

Ella Returns to Berlin (Verve Records)

WEBSITES:

EllaFitzgerald.com. Biography. Accessed
June 29, 2022. ellafitzgerald.com/about
/biography.

History.com editors. "Ella Fitzgerald Wins
Amateur Night at Harlem's Apollo Theater."
Last modified November 19, 2020. history
.com/this-day-in-history/ella-fitzgerald-wins
-amateur-night-at-harlems-apollo-theater.

Wong, Hannah. Library of Congress. "First
Lady of Song." Accessed June 29, 2022.
loc.gov/loc/lcib/9708/ella.html.

Kuske, Rebecca. National Museum of American
    History. April 1, 2017. "Ella Fitzgerald:
    Breaking Down Racial Barriers with Her
    Voice. americanhistory.si.edu/blog/ella
    -fitzgerald-voice.

Gleason, Holly. NPR.org. "The Joy of Ella
    Fitzgerald's Accessible Elegance." September
    5, 2019. npr.org/2019/09/05/749021799/the
    -joy-of-ella-fitzgeralds-accessible-elegance.

ANDREA DAVIS PINKNEY is the *New York Times* bestselling and award-winning author of numerous books for children and young adults, and has been recognized by the Coretta Scott King Author Award committee with an honor for *Let It Shine: Stories of Black Women Freedom Fighters* and a medal for *Hand in Hand: Ten Black Men Who Changed America*. She is a four-time nominee for the NAACP Image Award. In addition to her work as an author, Ms. Pinkney is a publishing executive. She has been named one of the "25 Most Influential Black Women" by *The Network Journal*, and is among *Children's Health* magazine's "25 Most Influential People in Our Children's Lives."

You can follow Andrea Davis Pinkney on Twitter
@AndreaDavisPink
on Instagram
@AndreaPinkney1
and on Facebook

GILLIAN FLINT has worked as a professional illustrator since earning an animation and illustration degree in 2003. Her work has since been published in the UK, USA and Australia. In her spare time, Gillian enjoys reading, spending time with her family and puttering about in the garden on sunny days. She lives in the northwest of England.

Courtesy of the illustrator

You can visit Gillian Flint online at
gillianflint.com
or follow her on Twitter
@GillianFlint
and on Instagram
@gillianflint_illustration

CHELSEA CLINTON is the author of the #1 *New York Times* bestseller *She Persisted: 13 American Women Who Changed the World*; *She Persisted Around the World: 13 Women Who Changed History*; *She Persisted in Sports: American Olympians Who Changed the Game*; *Don't Let Them Disappear: 12 Endangered Species Across the Globe*; *It's Your World: Get Informed, Get Inspired & Get Going!*; *Start Now!: You Can Make a Difference*; with Hillary Clinton, *Grandma's Gardens* and *Gutsy Women*; and, with Devi Sridhar, *Governing Global Health: Who Runs the World and Why?* She is also the Vice Chair of the Clinton Foundation, where she works on many initiatives, including those that help empower the next generation of leaders. She lives in New York City with her husband, Marc, their children and their dog, Soren.

You can follow Chelsea Clinton on Twitter
@ChelseaClinton
or on Facebook at
facebook.com/chelseaclinton

ALEXANDRA BOIGER has illustrated nearly twenty picture books, including the She Persisted books by Chelsea Clinton; the popular Tallulah series by Marilyn Singer; and the Max and Marla books, which she also wrote. Originally from Munich, Germany, she now lives outside of San Francisco, California, with her husband, Andrea, daughter, Vanessa, and two cats, Luiso and Winter.

You can visit Alexandra Boiger online at
alexandraboiger.com
or follow her on Instagram
@alexandra_boiger

Read about more inspiring women in the

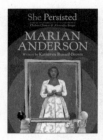

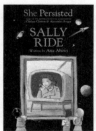
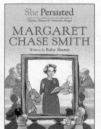

She Persisted series!

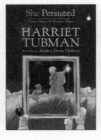